SUNS & MOONS

SUNS & MOONS

LINDSAY PORTER

PHOTOGRAPHS BY DEBBIE PATTERSON

LORENZ BOOKS

LONDON • NEW YORK • SYDNEY • BATH

Picture Credits
The publishers would like to thank e t archive for the pictures on page 8 (top) and 11
(bottom), Archive Für Kunst Und Geschichte for the pictures on pages 8/9 (centre) and
10 (bottom), Images for the picture on page 10 (top) and The Fortean Picture Library for the
picture on page 11 (bottom).

First published in 1996 by Lorenz Books

Lorenz Books is an imprint of
Anness Publishing Limited
Boundary Row Studios
1 Boundary Row
London SE1 8HP

This edition is distributed in Canada by
Raincoast Books Distribution Limited

ISBN 1 85967 139 X

Publisher: Joanna Lorenz
Assistant Editor: Sarah Ainley
Copy Editor: Deborah Savage
Designer: Lilian Lindblom
Step Photographer: Lucy Tizard
Illustrator: Lucinda Ganderton
Introduction by Tessa Evelegh

Printed in Singapore by
Star Standard Industries Pte Ltd

Contents

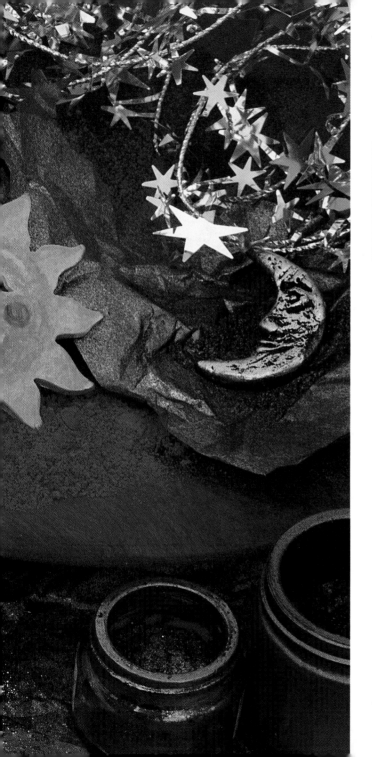

INTRODUCTION

Since man first looked skywards, he's been inspired by the sun and moon, with most societies lending them a religious significance. The Bible itself makes many mentions of the significance of the sun and moon, but although it frequently refers to New Moon Festivals and Sabbath Days (literally Sun Days), these are seen as an opportunity to worship their Maker rather than to worship the sun and moon themselves. The worship of heavenly bodies has been left to pagan religions, but that does not lessen their symbolism in the collective consciousness. The sun, particularly, being the source of heat and light, and therefore of life to the whole world, has been seen as a god by many peoples over the ages: the Babylonians and Assyrians worshipped the sun god Shamash; the Persians, Mithras; the Egyptians, Ra; the Aztecs, Tezcatlipoca; the Greeks, Helios, and the Romans, Sol. The moon's waxing and waning has been a source of intrigue to cultures since time began, with the horns facing east as it waxes, and west as it wanes on the way to becoming a full circle again.

The moon was seen as a time measure, and even its name may be connected with the Sanskrit root "me", to measure, so called because it measured the passing of each month. The moon's ability to control the tides was also seen as gracing it with mystical powers. This fascination with suns and moons meant they have always held a significance in art and decoration. As well as the obvious ancient connections, they appear in many Christian religious paintings. Sun and moon motifs can be seen in ancient carvings, stone and metalwork; on wallpaper and decorations for the home.

Even without mystical significance, sun and moon represent day and night. The ruler of the day – the sun – signifies bright optimism,and the symbol of the night – the moon – is symbolic of the peace of the night. Traditionally, both celestial bodies have been given a

Above: Nefertiti adoring solar disc from Tell el Amarna Kingdom, 18th Dynasty, Egypt.

Right: 19th-century German wood carvings.

personality, either through a pagan deity, or through folklore, where the sun and moon were endowed with a gender. For the ancient Slavs and Mexicans the sun was female and the moon male. So it still is with the Lithuanians, and the Germans, who call the sun Frau Sonne (Mrs Sun) and the moon Herr Mond (Mr Moon). This means the sun and moon can be personalized by giving them faces and expressions. These can range from cartoon-like nursery rhyme illustrations to almost godlike features in stone or wood carvings, and even metalwork. But whatever their significance,these heavenly bodies make perfect motifs for decorative work as they are simple forms that are easy to copy, even for children. But simplicity need not preclude creativity. Suns can have rays that are large or small, straight or wavy, regular or irregular. Moons can be round or crescent, slim or generous. The sun is a favourite motif in quite surprising crafts. For example, there is a great tradition for it in quilting with typical patchwork patterns being Sun, Sunburst or Rising Sun, in which tiny pieces, often diamond shaped, are pieced together. The single sunburst, which is one large sun motif taking up most or all of the quilt, is traditionally seen as the ultimate in accomplished quilting. Worked from the centre outwards, it requires accurate cutting and stitching if the sunburst is not to become mis-shapen. This ancient sunburst symbol was a favourite amongst settlers in the new world: they often painted their barns with splashy sun shapes – icons brought from their old countries.

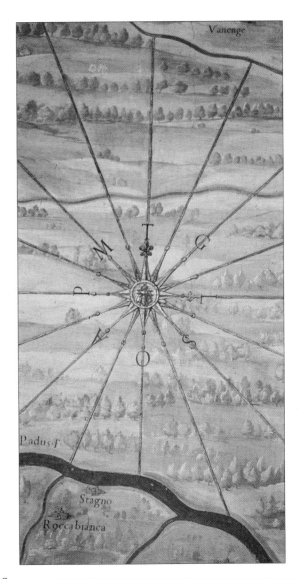

Right: Rays of the Sun, from the Gallery of Maps, commissioned by Gregory XIII, 1580-83.

Above: Personification of the Moon in a boat, holding the lunar crescent and accompanied with the sign Cancer. Statuary detail from the Doge's Palace, Venice.

Suns and moons can be used as single eye-catching motifs, grouped with stars, or used tiny in appealing all-over designs. This works particularly well for fabric and wallpaper printing, tapestries and embroideries.

Below: Frau Sonne, 19th-century German woodcarving.

Although, like any motif, suns and moons can be used in any colour, it seems that custom dictates they're happiest in shades that range from white through yellow to rich golds and silvers. Their suitability for the metallic tones makes them perfect motifs for richly adorned pieces in all media, from gold, silver and bronze metal threads in embroidery, to striking jewellery in a range of metals.

Blues, indigos and purples are traditionally favourite background colours for suns and moons, representing the sky during the day and at night, but there is no reason why you should stick to these any more than you should stick to the traditional silvers, creams, yellows and golds for the motifs themselves. These distinctive shapes can easily hold their own in any colour. Sometimes, an unexpected colour can strengthen the image of the motif itself, lending it a fresh feel. Another way to give a new look to these motifs is to make them up in alternative materials. Try creating door or wall decorations for indoors or out using plant material. Make a willow frame, then weave in newly cut young stems of buddleia or clematis, and let them dry out *in situ*. Or bend sun and moon shapes from wire for robust yet intricate wall decorations. Here are just a few ideas to inspire your creativity. The pages of this book bring some of these ideas to life with clear, easy to follow instructions.

Left: Yarn painting of the Huichol Indians from central Mexico: a shaman (upper left) can direct the life force, represented as the sun shining over a corn field.

Below: 17th-century tiled panel from Portugal.

SUNBURST PAPIER-MACHE BOWL

This spectacular sun seems to burst out of the bowl towards you. Use all your creativity to make the design as exuberant as possible. Papier-mâché gives you the ability to make graceful vessels without the skill and equipment needed for making ceramics; this bowl is ideal for fruit, nuts or small display items, but you might well want to leave it empty to show it off.

YOU WILL NEED

MATERIALS
petroleum jelly
newspaper
PVA glue
white undercoat paint
gouache or acrylic paints:
  yellow, blue and red
gold "liquid leaf" paint or gold
  gouache paint
fixative spray
gloss varnish

FOR THE PAPIER-MACHE PULP
5 sheets newspaper
5 dessertspoons PVA glue
2 dessertspoons wallpaper paste
1 dessertspoon plaster of Paris
1 dessertspoon linseed oil

EQUIPMENT
bowl for mould
paint-mixing container
medium and fine paintbrushes
pair of compasses
pencil

TO MAKE THE PAPIER-MACHE PULP
Tear the paper into pieces about 2.5 cm/1 in square and put them in an old saucepan with water to cover. Simmer for about 30 minutes. Spoon the paper and any water into a blender and liquidize it. Pour into a suitable container (lidded plastic boxes, such as ice-cream boxes, are ideal, because the pulp keeps for several weeks). Add the PVA glue, wallpaper paste, plaster of Paris and lin-seed oil. Stir vigorously and the pulp is ready to use.

1 Apply a coat of petroleum jelly to the inside of the bowl you are using as a mould. Tear strips of newspaper and, after dipping them in water, lay them over the inside of the mould.

2 Press the pulp into the mould so it's about 1 cm/ ½ in thick. Leave to dry in an airing cupboard, which will take about five days.

3 Release the dried pulp from the mould and cover it in strips of newspaper that you have dipped in PVA glue. Leave to dry.

4 Give the bowl two coats of white undercoat, allowing each coat to dry.

5 Use the pair of compasses to locate the sun shape accurately; first draw a small circle for the centre and then a larger one to contain the rays. Draw the rays freehand.

6 First fill in the yellow and gold areas. Paint the rim in gold. Fill in the blue background, leaving a white band below the gold rim.

7 Finally, paint the red border and allow to dry. Seal the bowl with fixative spray. Protect it with a coat of varnish.

SUN-GILDED BOX

A gilded sun graces the lid of a plain wooden box with a touch of celestial mystery. This luxurious effect is easily achieved using Dutch gold leaf. Delineate the gilding area with size, to provide an adhesive background, then apply the Dutch gold as a transfer.

YOU WILL NEED

MATERIALS
wooden box
acrylic gesso
ultramarine acrylic paint
gloss varnish
Japanese gold size
Dutch gold leaf transfer book
silver leaf transfer book

EQUIPMENT
paint-mixing container
medium and fine paintbrushes
sandpaper

1 Paint the box, inside and out, with three or more coats of acrylic gesso, using a medium brush (too many coats may stop the lid from closing properly, so be careful). Leave to dry thoroughly.

2 Give the box a coat of ultramarine acrylic paint, using a fine brush. When dry, lightly sand to give a distressed effect. Add a coat of varnish.

3 Paint a freehand sun motif on the lid, using the fine brush and the gold size. When the surface is just tacky, place the gold leaf transfer on top and rub gently with a finger.

Using the same technique, paint loose, freehand moons around the sides of the box and the side of the lid. Apply silver leaf transfer and leave to dry thoroughly.

HEAVENLY TIMEPIECE

This clock, decorated with a découpaged print of an antique map of the heavens, combines practicality with a reminder of the timeless mystery of the stars. The luxurious gilded finish enhances the atmosphere created by the map; hang the clock where it will catch the light and create a mood of serenity and contemplation.

YOU WILL NEED

MATERIALS
*hardboard, 30 x 30 cm/
  12 x 12 in
celestial map print
Japanese gold size
Dutch gold leaf transfer book
all-purpose glue
clock workings and hands*

EQUIPMENT
*pencil
ruler
scissors
drill, with size 10 bit
paintbrush*

1 Using the pencil and ruler, draw two diagonals across the hardboard, to find the centre of the square. Cut out the celestial map and find its centre in the same way. Place the map on the hardboard, draw round the outside of the map, and remove it.

2 Drill a hole in the centre of the hardboard to fit the width of the clock mechanism. Paint a coat of size around the edge, up to the pencil line. Leave until touch-dry. Lay strips of gold leaf on top of the size to cover. Trim off any excess by rubbing with a finger.

3 Pierce a hole in the centre of the map for the hands. Stick the map in position.

4 Add the hands and the clock mechanism.

ASTROLOGICAL CUSHION

This cushion cover achieves its effect with a combination of metallic fabric and embroidery. The cover creates a rich and luxurious impression, but machine embroidery makes the cover relatively straight-forward to achieve. This cushion is bound to induce a feeling of tranquillity when you settle down for a nap.

YOU WILL NEED

MATERIALS
brown velvet
matching thread
matching zip
gold metallic organza
matching machine embroidery
  thread
tracing paper
press fasteners
cushion pad

EQUIPMENT
tape measure
scissors
vanishing fabric marker
sewing machine, with
  darning foot
embroidery hoop
needle

1 For the front, cut one piece of velvet to the size of the cushion pad plus 2 cm/¾ in all round. For the back, cut two pieces of velvet each to half the width of the front piece, plus a 2 cm/¾ in turning allowance on both centre-back edges. Join the two pieces and insert the zip. Lay the front and back right sides together and stitch all round the outside. Cut one front and two back pieces of organza in the same way. Turn under and stitch a double hem of 1 cm/½ in on each centre edge of the back pieces.

Trace the template from the back of the book and enlarge it to size, if necessary. Put the front organza piece over the design and trace it on to the fabric with a fabric marker.

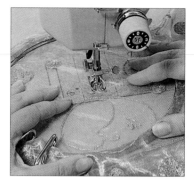

2 On the sewing machine, select the darning or free-embroidery mode. Place the organza in an embroidery hoop and then stitch round the shapes with gold embroidery thread.

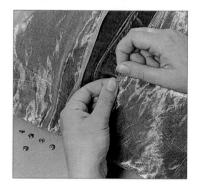

3 With right sides facing, stitch the organza pieces together. Stitch on the press fasteners. Insert the cushion pad in the velvet and insert the cushion in the organza.

MIDNIGHT-SKY EMBROIDERED PICTURE

Glittering metallic threads against shimmering dark blue shot silk create a real feeling of the night sky in this picture, which combines appliqué and machine-embroidery techniques. If you hang it above your bed, it will be like gazing through a magical window at night.

YOU WILL NEED

MATERIALS
pearlized chiffon and lamé
dark blue shot silk, about
  23 x 23 cm/9 x 9 in
machine embroidery thread:
  metallic silver, gold and blue
wadding
thick card
all-purpose glue

EQUIPMENT
pencil
thin card
scissors
vanishing fabric marker
embroidery hoop
ruler
dressmaker's pins
sewing machine, with
  darning foot

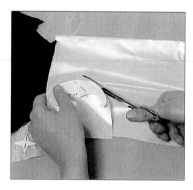

1 Draw the moon and stars freehand on to thin card and cut out to use as templates. Draw round the templates on the pearlized fabrics, using the fabric marker, and cut them out.

2 Stretch the silk in an embroidery hoop. Mark out a 10 cm/4 in square in the centre, using the fabric marker. Position the pearlized shapes and pin them in place.

3 Using metallic thread and with the machine on the darning or free-embroidery mode, define the shapes with machine embroidery. Continue building up colours and layers.
  Take the piece out of the hoop. Cut 10 cm/4 in squares of wadding and thick card. Lay the embroidery face down and place the wadding and card on top. Glue the edges of the card and then stretch the silk over and press it down firmly. Add a few stitches to hold the silk.

NIGHT AND DAY MOBILE

Golden suns and moody blue moons contrast with one another in this attractive mobile. Although mobiles are usually associated with children's rooms, this one is sophisticated enough to hang up as a decoration in any room in the house.

YOU WILL NEED

MATERIALS
corrugated card
newspaper
masking tape
wallpaper paste
small brass screw hooks
epoxy resin glue
PVA glue
white undercoat paint
gouache paints: blue, silver,
* orange, red and white*
gloss and matt varnishes
gold enamel paint
small jewellery jump rings
picture-hanging wire

EQUIPMENT
pencil
craft knife
medium and fine paintbrushes
paint-mixing container

1 Draw all the freehand shapes on the corrugated card and cut them out with a sharp craft knife.

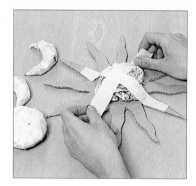

2 Bulk out the shapes by scrunching up pieces of newspaper, wrapping masking tape around them to secure them in place.

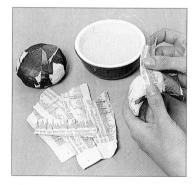

3 Cover the pieces in several layers of newspaper strips soaked in wallpaper paste. Allow to dry overnight, or longer if necessary.

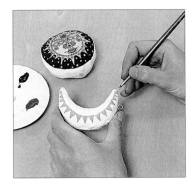

4 Screw in the hooks in the appropriate places for hanging, securing them with epoxy resin.

5 Coat the shapes with PVA glue and allow to dry. Coat with white undercoat and leave to dry again.

6 Mix the gouache paints to make a range of colours and decorate the shapes.

7 Give the shapes several coats of gloss varnish, picking out some areas in matt varnish, to contrast. Allow to dry. Add details in gold enamel, painted on with a fine brush.

8 Assemble all the pieces, using the hooks and jump rings to join them together. Suspend the mobile from a length of picture wire threaded through the hook and ring in the topmost shape.

SUN-SHAPED GOLDEN MIRROR

The glittering contrasts of gold paint and the warm, metallic hues of copper combine to flattering effect in this mirror frame. The curvaceous shapes in twisted wire set off the graphic copper triangles to create a really stylish effect that will be at home in any contemporary décor.

YOU WILL NEED

MATERIALS
copper sheet
copper wire
modelling clay
small round mirror
terracotta acrylic paint
gold powder
matt varnish
hanging fixture

EQUIPMENT
tin snips
ruler
wire cutters
jeweller's pliers
rolling pin
modelling tools
paint-mixing container
medium paintbrushes

1 Cut out six triangles from the copper sheet. Cut the wire into twelve 25 cm/10 in lengths. With the pliers, bend six wires into zigzags and six wires into spirals.

2 Roll the clay to 5 mm/¼ in thick. Cut out two 13 cm/ 5 in circles. Cut a 6 cm/2½ in circle from the centre of one. Place the mirror in the centre of the other and the wires and triangles around the edge.

3 Place the second clay circle on top and smooth the edges together with a wet modelling tool. Leave to dry for 2–3 days.

4 Paint the clay with terracotta acrylic paint. Leave to dry. Mix the gold powder with the varnish. Paint over the terracotta and attach a hanging fixture.

SUN AND MOON GARDEN STICKS

These cheerful sun and moon faces are very simple to make and will really brighten up the garden. Use them to enhance the festive atmosphere when you are having a barbecue or garden party. You could also put them into a border or bed, or use them to give height and structure to plants in a container.

YOU WILL NEED

MATERIALS
5 mm/¼ in thick birch-faced
  plywood sheet
garden sticks or canes
white undercoat paint
PVA glue
acrylic paints: red, yellow, brown,
  blue, white and silver
gloss varnish

EQUIPMENT
pencil
tracing paper
coping saw or fretsaw
medium- and fine-grade
  sandpaper
drill, with size 8 bit
paint-mixing container
medium and fine paintbrushes

1 Draw the sun and moon shapes freehand on to tracing paper and transfer the outlines to the plywood. Cut out the shapes with the saw and sand the edges smooth. Drill a hole in the edge of each shape for the sticks.

2 Paint the sticks and shapes all over with undercoat. Allow to dry. Sand lightly with fine-grade sandpaper. Glue the sticks in place.

3 Decorate with acrylic paints and leave to dry. Finish with a coat of varnish.

GOLD BAS-RELIEF CANDLE JARS

Use the brilliant colours of glass paints and gold outliner to create a rich and luminous effect that will make the most of candle-light. The outliner gives a relief design with an almost Indian feel. It's easier to paint the jars with the background colour before applying the outliner, unless you want to use several colours of glass paint on the same piece. In this case, use the outliner to make your design and, when it's completely dry, paint the colours on with a fine brush, taking care not to let the paint get on the relief work.

YOU WILL NEED

MATERIALS
jars
methylated spirits
solvent-based glass paints
gold glass-painting outliner

EQUIPMENT
medium paintbrush
kitchen paper

1 Wash the jars in hot soapy water to remove any grease and residue from the labels. Use methylated spirits to remove any stubborn bits. Dry the jars thoroughly. Using the glass paint straight from the jar, paint the jars generously. The viscous texture of the paint allows it to run fairly slowly, to give even cover, but do not let heavy drips build up because the paint dries quickly. Most brushmarks will fade as the paint dries. Leave to dry for about 24 hours.

2 Apply the designs with the outliner. Start with the border at the top and bottom. Mistakes can be quickly wiped away with kitchen paper.

3 Now fill in the motifs in the middle. The outliner takes a very long time to dry completely; though it is touch-dry within 24 hours, allow up to 72 hours to be really sure.

CELESTIAL WRAPPING PAPER

Red and gold suns grace a midnight-blue background to create a sheet of wrapping paper that will be as special as the present you wrap in it. If you can't bear to part with the paper when you've finished making it, use it to cover a box such as a hatbox. You could experiment with other colour combinations.

YOU WILL NEED

MATERIALS
acrylic paints: gold and red
white paper
acetate sheet
masking tape
plain blue wrapping paper

EQUIPMENT
2 paint-mixing dishes or plates
small paint roller
sun-motif rubber stamp
self-healing cutting mat
craft knife
stencil brush
newspaper

1 To make the stencil for the dropped shadow effect, put a little gold paint on a dish and roll the paint on to the stamp. Stamp a sun on the white paper. Put the paper on the cutting mat, place the acetate on top and secure with masking tape. Cut out the sun outline with a craft knife. Place the stencil on the wrapping paper and secure with masking tape.

2 Put some red paint on another dish and dip in the stencil brush, dabbing off any excess on to newspaper. Stipple the paint on to the wrapping paper through the stencil. Repeat, moving the acetate and re-securing it, until the whole paper is covered in an orderly and spacious pattern of suns.

3 Put some more gold paint on the dish and roll the paint on to the stamp. Stamp the design on top of the red suns, as closely as possible to the original outline, to give a three-dimensional effect.

SUN AND MOON BADGES

Wear one of these jolly badges as a colourful and bold brooch on a plain coat or sweater. Simple to make, these badges are bound to lift your spirits in the morning.

YOU WILL NEED

MATERIALS
5 mm/¼ in thick birch-faced plywood sheet
white undercoat paint
acrylic paints: yellow, red and blue
gloss varnish
epoxy resin or hot glue
2 brooch pins

EQUIPMENT
pencil
coping saw or fretsaw
medium- and fine-grade sandpaper
paint-mixing container
medium and fine paintbrushes

1 Trace the templates from the back of the book, enlarge them to size and transfer the outlines to the plywood. Cut out the shapes with the saw and sand the edges smooth.

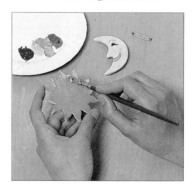

2 Paint both sides and all the edges of the shapes with white undercoat. When the paint is dry, sand it lightly.

3 Paint the fronts of the sun and moon with acrylic paint and add the features and other details. When the paint is dry, add a coat of varnish and leave to dry. Put a thick line of glue on the back of each badge and press the brooch pin firmly into the glue.

SUNS AND MOONS STENCILLED NAPKINS

Transform plain white napkins by decorating them with golden suns and blue moons. To achieve the best result, cut the stencils carefully and take great care in registering them accurately, with the help of the cross-points you draw on the napkin. Have a spare blade to hand, as a sharp knife will be essential.

YOU WILL NEED

MATERIALS
2 sheets of stencil card, as large as the napkins
thick card
spray adhesive
napkins
fabric paints: gold and blue

EQUIPMENT
pencil
ruler
craft knife
self-healing cutting mat
iron
vanishing fabric marker
sponge or stencil brush

1 Trace the design from the back of the book and enlarge it, if necessary. Rule grids on the stencil card to help you position the motifs. Transfer the motifs on to the stencil card; you will need to make one stencil for the suns and one for the moons. Cut out the stencils.

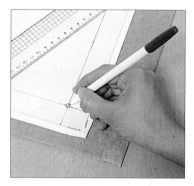

2 Apply spray adhesive to the sun stencil. Iron a napkin. Lay the napkin right side up on the thick card and smooth it outwards from the centre. With a fabric marker, draw the registration marks on the napkin, parallel to the edges. The registration lines should cross at the centre of the corner sun motif.

3 Apply spray adhesive to the reverse of the sun stencil and register the stencil over the napkin. Using a sponge or stencil brush, apply the gold paint. Remove the stencil, then leave to dry. Repeat with the moon stencil and blue paint, registering the stencil as before. When dry, iron on the back to fix the paint.

BEAMING SUN WALL PLAQUE

A cheerful sunny face looking down at you is sure to cheer you up, so put this wall plaque where it will do you most good – perhaps over the breakfast table! The plaque is made from sandwiched layers of corrugated card and mounted on card in the same way, so it's very easy to make. There is also an alternative idea using papier-mâché pulp to mould the face.

YOU WILL NEED

MATERIALS
corrugated card
newspaper or masking tape
PVA glue
white undercoat paint
acrylic paints: red, yellow
  and blue
matt varnish

EQUIPMENT
pair of compasses
pencil
scissors
paint-mixing container
medium paintbrushes

1 Draw and cut five equal circles of card to the required size. Glue together three circles. Bind the edges with newspaper strips dipped in PVA glue, or with masking tape.

2 Glue the remaining two circles together and cut out a circle from their centre. Trim this smaller circle so there will be a gap all round it when it's replaced. This forms the face at the centre of the plaque.

3 On the circle with the hole, draw the rays of the sun. Cut them out. Bind the edges inside and out and also the edges of the small circle.

4 Glue the sun rays and the face on to the backing circle, centring the face in the slightly larger area left for it.

5 Draw the features on card freehand and cut them out. Glue them on to the face.

6 Prime the whole of the plaque with white under-coat and leave to dry.

7 Decorate with acrylic paints. When dry, apply two coats of varnish.

8 Alternatively, make the sun shape from papier-mâché pulp, as described for the Sunburst Papier-mâché Bowl, moulding it by hand on the backing circle. Use fine string to delineate the features and give relief detail to the rays. Coat the face in primer and paint as before.

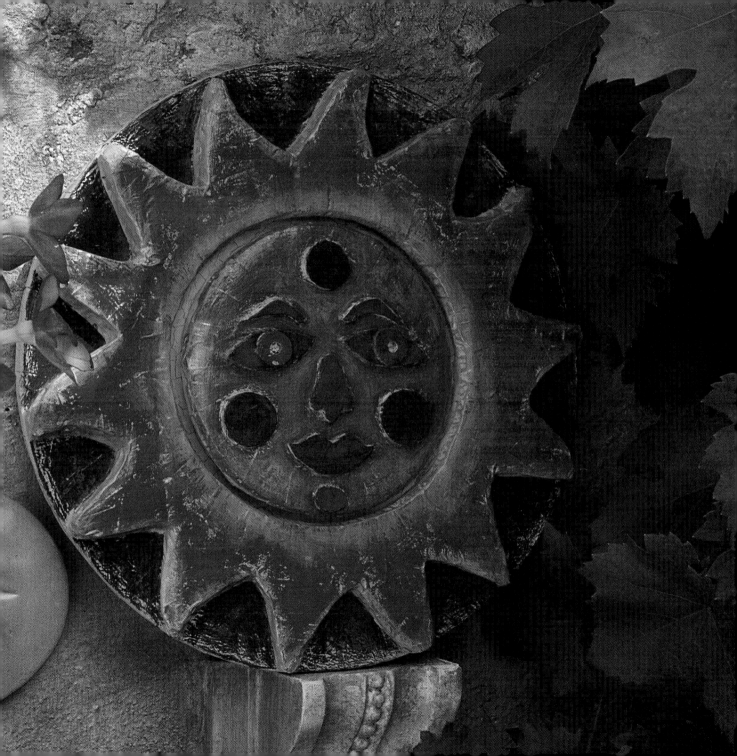

SUN AND MOON EARRINGS

These very striking earrings shimmer with a distressed black and gold paint effect that is simple to achieve but looks stunning. The faces are easily modelled out of clay and you only need to leave them to dry thoroughly before you paint them, for a durable finish. The earrings would enhance any formal, especially black, outfit, or add a touch of glamour to casual clothes.

YOU WILL NEED

MATERIALS
modelling clay
strong clear glue
2 earring "findings" (backs and
 butterflies) for pierced ears
black acrylic paint
gold powder
matt varnish

EQUIPMENT
rolling pin
jar lid
modelling tools
fine-grade sandpaper
paint-mixing container
fine paintbrushes

1 Roll out two pieces of clay to a circle about 5 mm/¼ in thick and 8 cm/3 in diameter. Use the jar lid as a template to mark an inner circle. With a modelling tool, build up the central area so it is higher than the outer area but still flat.

2 Model the features of your sun with a modelling tool. Mark the rays around the face and cut away the excess clay. Pierce some dots in the face and rays and leave to dry for 1–2 days. Model a moon in the same way.

3 Glue the earring backs in position. Sand between the rays for a smoother look. Paint black. Mix the gold powder with the varnish, then paint. With a semi-dry brush, go over the face up and down quickly, so that the black underneath shows through and accentuates the features of the face.

HEAVENLY BODIES HAT

This richly coloured hat is made from a circle and a rectangle. Measure your head and add a 5 cm/2 in seam and shrinkage allowance. The height of the hat shown is 12 cm/4¾ in plus a 2.5 cm/1 in seam allowance. Cut a circle for the top according to the size required, plus a 2.5 cm/1 in seam allowance.

YOU WILL NEED

MATERIALS
dupion silk in 3 colours
heavy iron-on interfacing
10 cm/4 in square velvet
contrasting cotton threads
contrasting metallic machine-
  embroidery threads
metallic fabric paints

EQUIPMENT
tape measure
ruler
scissors
sewing machine, with
  darning foot
dressmaker's pins
pencil
medium paintbrush

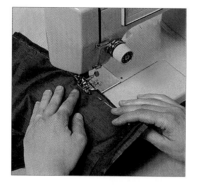

2 Draw and cut out sun and moon shapes and pin on to the silk. With the machine in embroidery mode, stitch on top of the moon template, then stitch the features. Stitch the stars and outline stitching in the same way, using different coloured threads. Go over all the stitching twice. Tear away the paper.

1 Cut three rectangles of silk and one of interfacing to the correct size. Iron the interfacing on to the back of the bottom layer of silk. Stitch around the edge of the rectangles, leaving a gap in one long seam. Insert a square of velvet through the gap, on top of the top layer of silk and pin in place.

3 Next, cut out the fabric layers to reveal your desired colours. Random whip stitch in a loop fashion inside the moon, with metallic thread. Paint areas of the hat with metallic fabric paints. Stitch the crown and top of the hat together and clip into the seam allowances.

PAINTED SILK SCARF

Reminiscent of the stained-glass rose windows that are such a breath-taking feature of medieval churches and cathedrals, this design is created by making outlines of gutta and painting in between them. Bought silk scarves are useful for this project, because the edges are ready-rolled. Any kind of frame can be used for stretching, as long as it is large and strong enough to hold the silk completely stretched and flat.

YOU WILL NEED

MATERIALS
silk square
gutta
silk paints: selection of colours

EQUIPMENT
frame
dressmaker's pins
vanishing fabric marker
pipette
fine-pointed watercolour
  paintbrush
iron

1 Wash the silk to remove all impurities and finish the edges if necessary. Stretch and pin the silk on to the frame.

2 Draw out your chosen design on to the silk, using a fabric marker.

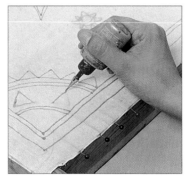

3 Apply the gutta, using the pipette. Make sure you press firmly and squeeze at the same time. It is important for the gutta line to be solid, to prevent the paint from bleeding. Always check for any gaps. Leave the gutta to dry.

4 After the gutta has dried, apply the silk paints. Leave to dry. Carefully remove the silk from the frame and iron it for five minutes.

EMBROIDERED HATPIN

A decorated hatpin is an easy way to jazz up a plain hat. This one features an elaborately embroidered velvet sun backed with beaten brass.

YOU WILL NEED

MATERIALS
yellow velvet
fine strong fabric
contrasting cotton threads
contrasting metallic machine-
* embroidery threads*
brass sheet
brass wire
epoxy resin glue
beads
hatpin

EQUIPMENT
scissors
embroidery hoop
sewing machine, with
* darning foot*
tin snips
metal file
small, round-nosed hammer
wire cutters
round-nosed jeweller's pliers

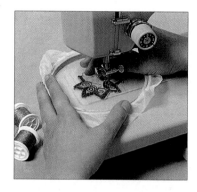

1 Cut out a yellow velvet sun. Place a piece of fine fabric in an embroidery hoop and machine-stitch the sun to it. Thread the machine with contrasting threads in the top and bobbin and whip stitch around the edge. Then make a deeper band of stitching around the edge. Stitch spirals in contrasting metallic threads, then stitch the face.

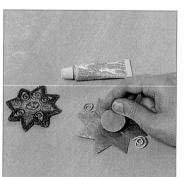

2 Cut a sun from the brass sheet with tin snips and file the edges smooth. Hammer to give texture. Bend a spiral at each end of a piece of wire and hammer flat. Position the wire spirals in the centre front of the sun shape and glue a circle of brass just in the centre, over the ends of the wire.

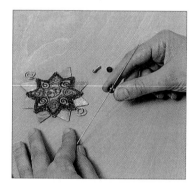

3 Trim the velvet sun away from the fine fabric and glue it in the centre of the brass sun. Thread some beads on the hat pin and glue them in place. To assemble, bend the spirals slightly backwards and slide the hatpin through the top and bottom spirals.

ASTROLOGICAL DRAWSTRING BAG

This delicate and pretty bag in shimmering metallic organza would be ideal for lingerie. The technique is to outline the shapes with embroidery and then to cut away inside the shapes, so the silver organza shows though the gold. Metallic embroidery threads complement the fabric.

YOU WILL NEED

MATERIALS
*2 rectangles silver metallic
    organza, 65 x 28 cm/
    26 x 11 in*
*2 rectangles gold metallic
    organza, 24 x 28 cm/7 x 11 in*
*contrasting metallic machine-
    embroidery threads*
*2 circles silver metallic organza,
    18 cm/7 in diameter*
ribbon

EQUIPMENT
scissors
tape measure
*sewing machine, with
    darning foot*
needle and tacking thread
vanishing fabric marker
embroidery hoop

1 Fold the rectangular pieces in half widthways, right sides together. Stitch an 8 cm/3 in seam on both sides. Turn the rectangles right sides out. To make the ribbon casing, stitch two parallel lines 8 and 10 cm/ 3 and 4 in from the folded edge. Tack a gold rectangle to a silver rectangle, matching the bottom edges.

3 Cut away the gold organza inside the stitched line. Work the remaining signs in contrasting colours. Cut away and discard the organza again. Top-stitch 1.5 cm/⅝ in from the top edge and pull away the weft threads, to produce a gold fringe. Remove the tacking. Lay the two embroidered sides right sides together.

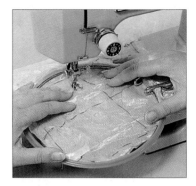

2 Using a fabric marker, trace the template from the back of the book on to the gold side of the two silver and gold pieces. On the sewing machine, set the dial to the darning or free-embroidery mode. Work the motifs in straight-stitch, with contrasting thread in the top and bobbin.

4 Stitch the side edges, start-ing at the lower casing seam, to make a tube-shaped outer, embroidered bag, with a lining formed by the folded half. Stitch one of the silver circles to the bottom of the outside tube, leaving a gap. Stitch the other to the bottom of the lining. Turn right-sides out. Tuck the lining inside the bag and slip-stitch the gap. Thread a ribbon through the casing.

SHINING SUN HATBOX

This hatbox positively glitters with gold decoration, creating an effect that seems to glow like the heavenly bodies it pays tribute to.

YOU WILL NEED

MATERIALS
carpet roll tube
card
masking tape
newspaper strips
PVA glue
white undercoat paint
acrylic paints: blue, deep violet
  red and yellow
gold paint
sun-face motif print
glitter glue

EQUIPMENT
saw, if necessary
tape measure
pair of compasses
pencil
craft knife
medium, small and fine
  paintbrushes
scissors

1 Using a section of a carpet tube, cut with a saw for the cylindrical part of the box, or bend a piece of card into a cylinder. Draw and cut a circle of card for the base and another slightly larger circle for the lid. Assemble the base and sides and fix with masking tape. Bind the edge and the join with strips of newspaper and slightly watered-down PVA glue. Leave to dry.

2 To make the lid, cut a long narrow strip of card the length of the circumference of the lid, plus a small overlap. Bend the strip and fix it in position with masking tape.and bind the edge and joins with newspaper strips in the same way as the the base. Leave to dry.

3 Prime the base and lid with white undercoat paint.

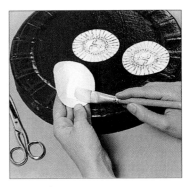

4 Mark the stripes on the side and paint them with different colours. Leave to dry. Use gold paint to add fine stripes.

5 Using gold paint and a fine paintbrush, carefully paint the fine details.

6 Paint the lid violet. Photocopy a motif about 18 times. Cut the photocopied motifs out and stick them to the lid and the side of the box, using watered-down PVA glue.

7 Paint the faces of the motifs to highlight the features and paint the backgrounds.

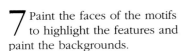

8 When dry, use glitter glue to add sparkle.

SUN JUG

A good way to brighten up a plain jug is to use china paints to apply a bold motif. This cheerful sun face would be particularly welcome on the breakfast table. The colours could be adapted to suit your other china.

YOU WILL NEED

MATERIALS
white ceramic jug
tracing paper
masking tape
acrylic china paints: black, bright yellow, ochre, blue, red and white

EQUIPMENT
hard and soft pencils
scissors
fine paintbrushes
hairdryer (optional)

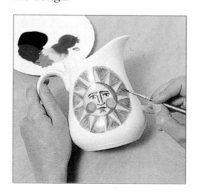

1 Wash the jug thoroughly to remove any grease. Trace the template and enlarge it, if necessary. Cut it out roughly and then rub over the back with a soft pencil. Make several cuts around the edge of the circle, so that the template will lie flat against the jug, and tape it in place. Draw over the outlines with a hard pencil to transfer the design.

2 Using and mixing the paints according to the manufacturer's instructions, paint the sun. Go over the outline for the features in black first of all and allow the black paint to dry completely; a hairdryer can speed up the drying process. Paint the main face and the inner rays in bright yellow and then paint the cheeks and the other parts of the rays in ochre.

3 Paint the background in blue and then add fine details to the sun face, to give it a sense of depth. Finish off by painting a white dot as a highlight in each eye. Bake in a medium oven, as directed by the paint manufacturer. The jug should withstand everyday use and gentle washing up, but not the dishwasher.

TEMPLATES

If the templates need to be enlarged, either use a grid system or a photocopier. For the grid system, trace the template and draw a grid of evenly spaced squares over your tracing. To scale up, draw a larger grid on to another piece of paper. Copy the outline on to the second grid by taking each square individually and drawing the relevant part of the outline in the larger square. For tracing templates you will need tracing paper, a pencil, card or paper and scissors.

Sun and Moon Badges, p36

Astrological Cushion and Astrological Drawstring Bag, pp 20 and 52

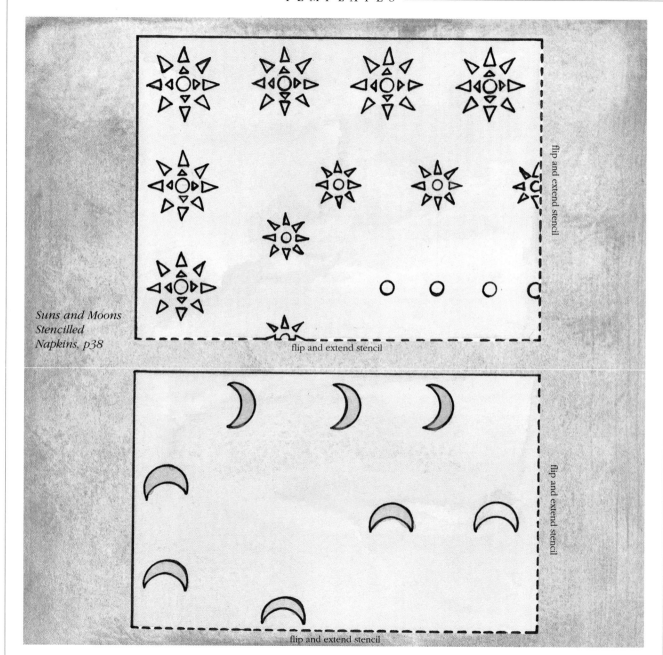

Suns and Moons Stencilled Napkins, p38

flip and extend stencil

flip and extend stencil

flip and extend stencil

flip and extend stencil

Sun Jug, p58

ACKNOWLEDGEMENTS

The author and publishers would like to thank the following people for designing the projects in this book:

Ofer Acoo
127 Northwold Road
London E5 8RL
Sun-shaped Golden Mirror pp28–29; Sun and Moon Earrings pp44–45

Madeleine Adams
Cobweb Cottage
Stourten Hill
Shipston on Stow
Warwicks CV36 5H14
Sunburst Papier-mâché Bowl pp12–15

Penny Boylan
13 Graveney Road
London SW17
Gold Bas-relief Candle Jars pp32–33

Judy Clayton
c/o the Publishers
Heavenly Bodies Hat pp46–47; Embroidered Hatpin pp50–51

Lucinda Ganderton
23 Albany Passage
The Alberts
Richmond, Surrey TW10 6DL
Sun Jug pp58–59

Louise Gardam
c/o Vena Bunker
24 Archfield Road
Cotham, Bristol BSG 6BE
Sun-gilded Box pp16–17

Jill Hancock
26 Park Road
Stonehouse
Glos GL10 2DE
Sun and Moon Garden Sticks pp30–31; Sun and Moon Badges pp36–37

Abigail Mill
Studio 10
Muspole Workshops
25–27 Muspole Street
Norwich, Norfolk NR3 1DJ
Midnight-sky Embroidered Picture pp22–23

Izzy Moreau
37 St James Park
Tunbridge Wells
Kent TN1 2LG
Beaming Sun Wall Plaque pp40–43; Shining Sun Hatbox pp54–56

Sarbjitt Natt
20 Elms Avenue
Muswell Hill
London N10
Suns and Moons Stencilled Napkins pp38–39; Painted Silk Scarf pp48–49

Kim Rowley
72 Clissold Crescent
London N16 9AT
Night and Day Mobile pp24–25

Isabel Stanley
5 Herne Hill Mansions
Herne Hill
London SE24
Astrological Cushion pp20–21; Astrological Drawstring Bag pp52–53

Josephine Whitfield
1 Chestnut Crescent
Aylesbury
Bucks HP21 8HX
Heavenly Timepiece pp18–19; Celestial Wrapping Paper pp34–35